Get Going

Transforming Passion into Performance and Productivity.

Sanjay Vishnu Bakle

BookLeaf Publishing

India | USA | UK

Made with ❤ on the BookLeaf Publishing Platform
www.bookleafpub.in
www.bookleafpub.com

Dedication

This book is dedicated to my incredible team, my colleagues, and the cross-functional members from other departments and locations. Throughout my journey in a fast-paced environment, where customer demand, satisfaction, and delight are paramount, I realized the power of inspiration and teamwork. To enhance the customer experience, I began coaching my team and finding new ways to uplift their spirit and drive excellence in everything they did. I learned that when proper direction is given, every individual is willing to go the extra mile.

In pursuit of this goal, I turned to poetry—capturing the essence of collaboration and the collective spirit that fuels our success. This collection is a reflection of that shared vision and the dedication that continues to inspire me.

Preface

Words have always been more than just a means of communication—they hold the power to connect, heal, and inspire. Having spent years in an environment where customer satisfaction is of the highest importance, I have witnessed how the right words can brighten someone's day, offer comfort, or spark motivation.

This collection of poetry is a reflection of that understanding—an attempt to capture emotions, experiences, and moments that resonate with the heart. Each verse is written with the hope that it finds a home in your thoughts, much like a kind word finds its way to those who need it most.

May these poems speak to you, uplift you, and remind you of the beauty in words and the power they hold.

Acknowledgements

I would like to extend my heartfelt gratitude to everyone who has played a part in bringing this book to life. First, I must thank my incredible team—your dedication, passion, and unwavering commitment to excellence inspired the very foundation of these poems. Without your enthusiasm and collaborative spirit, this book would not exist.

To my colleagues and cross-functional team members from other departments and locations, your support, cooperation, and shared vision have been invaluable.

Each of you has contributed to my growth, both personally and professionally, and for that, I am deeply grateful.

A special thanks to my mentors and coaches who have always believed in me and guided me with wisdom and patience. Your encouragement to look beyond the obvious and pursue my passions has been a gift.

Lastly, to my family and friends for their endless love, patience, and understanding—thank you for always being there and believing in me, even when the journey felt uncertain.

This book is a reflection of the collective energy, dedication, and spirit of everyone who has touched my life. Thank you all for being part of this journey.

With gratitude,
Sanjay Bakle

1. Fulfillment

Cherrish to flourish
Respect to respectful.
Hard to Honest
Great to Grateful
Make to Meaningful
Just to justice
Joy to Joyful
Fruit to Fruitful
Inspire to insightful.
Design too Delightful.
Mind to Mindful,
Grace to Graceful
Pace to Peaceful
Will to willful

2. Perception

Perception Prevails

Perceptions are not proof.
Perceptions can be permanent.
Perceptions can be presumptions.
Perceptions can be pro.
Perceptions can be past.
Perceptions can be present.
Perceptions can be predictive.
Perceptions may be pure.
Perceptions may be purposeful.
Perceptions are shaped by sight,
A fleeting truth, lost in the light.
They bend and twist, they cloud and veil,
Shifting, as the stories sail.
Perceptions may mislead the mind,
But through the lens, what truth will find?
They paint our world in shades so vast,
Ever-changing, from first to last.

3. Merit

Merit is a must,
Merit is a trust.
Merit is a boost,
Merit is thrust.
Merit is a nest,
Merit brings a net.
Merit brings zest,
Merit is the best.
Merit fuels the fire,
Lifts you higher.
Merit builds the way,
For a brighter day.
With merit as guide,
You'll never slide.
It carves your path,
Through every aftermath.
In merit, we rise,
With purpose in our eyes.
It's the spark in the soul,
That makes us whole.

4. Approach

Stay Cool
Stay Calm
Stay Basics
Stay Solutions
Stay Solid
Part Away Problem
Sow Seeds
Resolve Roots
Bear Fruits
Be Active
Not Reactive
Be inquisitive
Nil Repulsive
Radiate Rays
Of Respect
Never suspect
Gentle Acts
Open a gate
With thoughts
Revised focus

New locus
Change in range
Evolve in fringe
Never Mind
But be Kind.

5. Philosophy Journey

Philosophy Preaches,
Yet Experience Teaches.
Knowledge Enriches.
Intention Ignites.
Output intensifies.
Work Wonders,
Group Glorify.
Friendship Fosters.
The Next is new,
And New defines View,
New is Normal.
Past has Faded
Future is Fast,
Beginnings are beautiful.
Staying is successful,
Confidence Continues.
Learning is Legit.
Turning towards Truth,
Networking is Yearning!

6. Get Going

Gather your Team,
Align the Aim,
Gain the momentum.
Pain to Gain,
Full Train,
Mold the minds,
Suitable kinds,
Approach is in line,
Where customer is fine,
Focus is a sign.
Stretch your imagination,
Squeeze action time.
Move on mission,
Velocity to vision.
Get going,
Set Sowing,
Flourish & growing.
Nourish & Nurture,
That's the culture

7. Captain of Completion

Call colleagues,
Create connections,
Common Causes,
Concern corners,
Convey crisp,
Cultivate Creativity,
Communicate content,
Co-ordinate conversation,
Collect comments,
Champion change,
Combine crux,
Courageous Collaboration
Conformance to Consensus,
Crystal Clear,
Clean concepts
Camly Correct,
Course correction,
Cancel Convention,
Converging is current,
Compare & crystalize,

Credit cordially
Celebrate circumstances
Clap & Cherish
Conceive comfort
Commend Completion

8. Rise

Take steps.
Next phase,
No dread,
No mess,
Stay Blessed,
Slow pace,
Yet Progress,
Create space,
Work base,
Find your place,
Lead the race,
Quality chase
Customer face
Build that grace
Craft case
Neat & Nice
Only Choice
Strong poise
No Noise,
Bring up voice

Get the prize
Show up & rise.

9. Traction

Actions breed traction,
Traction fuels progression,
Progression grows in aggregation,
Aggregation ignites amplification,
Amplification leads to elevation,
Elevation brings forth vision,
Vision fuels the mission,
Mission drives multiplication,
Multiplication fosters conservation,
Conservation nurtures stabilization,
Stabilization strengthens standardization,
Standardization ensures continuation,
Continuation sparks competition,
Competition builds reliability,
Reliability drives reforms,
Reforms bring further traction!

10. Inside out and outside in

Let your work inside out,
Let your benchmark outside in!
Let your blessings inside out,
Let your prayers outside in!
Let your learning inside out,
Let your teachings outside in!
Let your intention inside out,
Let your adaptability outside in!
Let your sharing inside out,
Let your absorbing outside in!
Let your caring inside out,
Let your co-operation outside in!
Let your words inside out,
Let your statement outside in!
Let your care inside out,
Let your warmth outside in!
Let your passion inside out,
Let your energy outside in!
Let your dreams inside out,
Let your actions outside in!

Let your patience inside out,
Let your calmness outside in!
Let your vision inside out,
Let your focus outside in!
Let your hope inside out,
Let your faith outside in!
Let your creativity inside out,
Let your innovation outside in!
Let your strength inside out,
Let your resilience outside in!
Let your wisdom inside out,
Let your guidance outside in!
Let your joy inside out,
Let your laughter outside in!

11. Simplicity

When we gain, keep it humble,
When we lose, keep it straight,
When we are happy, keep it sharing,
When we are in pressure, keep it monitored,
When we are challenged, keep it as a chance,
When we are in trouble, keep it balanced,
When we are in hurry, keep out the worry,
When we are in need, keep it simple,
When we are upbeat, keep it spreading,
When we are in business, keep it profitable,
When we are reading, keep it focused,
When we are working, keep it flowing.

12. Champion

Backup or Backout
Set up over setback
Shine over shun
Fun over fury
Take it up or let it go
Embrace over isolate
Elevate over dilute
Choose with cheers
Throw out fears
That's the way to champion
Rise above the doubt,
Stand tall, no turning out.
Speak with purpose, loud and clear,
Chase the dream and persevere.
Move ahead, don't look behind,
Focus forward, strengthen mind.
Build with hope, and not regret,
Take the lead, don't break a sweat.
Power through and aim for more,
                   Open every single door.

13. Looking around

Looking back is reflection,
Looking forward is progression,
Looking ahead is vision,
Looking nowhere is confusion,
Looking all over is illusion,
Looking at right time is a choice,
Looking elsewhere is a noise,
Looking towards goal is a focus,
Looking and absorbing is a genius,
Looking and analyzing is a thinker,
Looking and spotting is capability,
Looking and working is a smart ability,
Looking and responding is responsive,
Overlooking is a mistake,
Looking within is introspection,
Looking with empathy is connection,
Looking with patience is understanding,
Looking with courage is daring,
Looking with love is caring,
Looking with hope is inspiring,

Looking with faith is believing !!

18

14. Prize of Teamwork

Words are worthy,
Thoughts are welcome,
Work is worship,
Hands are helpful,
Joining is joyous,
Support is a spirit,
Submission is super,
Connection is continuity,
Co-operation is contagious,
Co-ordination is concurrence,
Teamwork is testimony,
Unity is undivided,
Effort is endless,
Strength is shared,
Growth is collective,
Victory is ours,
Together we rise,
Teamwork is the ultimate prize.

15. Magnificient Mind

Strong mind sustains,
Determined mind delivers,
Ambitious mind achieves,
Open mind absorbs,
Active mind advances,
Positive mind shows progress,
Matured mind understands,
Focused mind directs
Curious mind explores
Resilient mind endures
Creative mind imagines
Compassionate mind connects
Patient mind waits
Wise mind guides
Clear mind sees
Balanced mind restores
Grateful mind appreciates

16. Peace of Mind

All life was a race,
Enjoyed the race with front face,
Challenges to maintain pace,
Searching for peace,
Thought it was a piece,
Places traveled,
People followed,
Work worshiped,
In the quiet of the night,
Found solace in the light,
Meditation and reflection,
Brought a new direction.
Through valleys deep
And mountains high,
Faced each challenge, reached the sky,
Struggles shaped the path we tread,
Lessons learned, no tears to shed.
In the heart, the truth resides,
Peace within, no need to hide,
Life's journey, though tough and long,

Rewards the soul, makes it strong.
Explored peace outside,
Finally realized peace is inside!

17. Unity Unites...

Promise what can be finished,
Co-operate for what's considered,
Cheers for what can be shared,
Grow where the team can grow,
Support where hands are open,
Manage where risk exists,
Coach where ears are hungry,
Respond where reciprocity repeats,
Sweat together to foster progress,
Work better, and results will be sweeter.
Build trust where the roots run deep,
Stand stronger when the storms are near,
Collaborate where silence speaks loud,
Lead where courage breaks the crowd,
Achieve together, step by step,
In unity, the future is kept.

18. Strength to Prevail

Smile takes you miles,
Good words are wise,
Work unites the world,
Nice work makes hearts swirl.
Prize the jewels of life,
Out comes the fragrance of strife.
Will to excel,
In unity, all gel.
Outcome shines,
Success aligns.
Nail each goal,
As you take control.
Easier the sail,

With strength to prevail
Cherish each day,
In every way.
Dreams take flight,
In the soft moonlight.

19. Work Flow

Work in a Flow,
Flow in Synchro,
Flow with a Glow,
Do not go Slow,
Keep the Pace,
In the Race,
Consistency is the Face,
Normal, not the Chase,
Work with Grace,
Keep up the Trace,
Tie up the Lace,
Firm the Brace,
Outcome will Raise,
Rise above the haze,
In victory, we'll praise.

20. Sports Person

Team spirit is the key we need,
It helps us rise and succeed.
Team spirit is an essential ingredient,
It helps us climb every gradient.
All challenges are transient,
Sportsmanship is urgent,
A trait that is truly emergent.
Through the game, our spirits lift,
It's what turns mere players into a team with grit.
Longing for that winning streak,
Where every victory feels unique.
Winning or losing, both part of the game,
A true sportsman rises, undeterred by fame.
A team can achieve the extraordinary,
By working together, that's the commentary.
Exemplary in all they do,
Their effort, dedication shining through.
The team can transform with every play,
Through hard work, they forge the way.
Sport is the ultimate stress-breaker,

The team, a result-maker, quicker and greater.
When we play, we don't just compete,
We unite, our hearts beat in the same beat.
Every pass, every goal, a shared dream,
Together we rise, together we gleam.
Sportsmanship builds a character,
That's the biggest differentiating factor!

21. Strength in Fear

Bank on fear
Live with care
Path is clear
Actions to Steer
Handle all gear
Work with dear
Finish with Shear
Goal is near
Continue lever
Nothing to bear
Success Superior,
Stand tall through doubt,
Push forward with grace.
Every step matter,
In this relentless race.
Strength in your soul,
Drive in your vein,
Success comes to those
Who endure through the strain.
Rise from the ashes,

Soar to new heights,
With courage as fuel,
You'll conquer the nights.